Time Management 101
for Students:

101 Tested and True Techniques to Take Charge of the Time of Your Life

For busy college and college-bound
students who want
to do well in school and still
have time for a balanced life.

Crystal Jonas

ISBN: 9780976934479

LCCN: 2006901114

Text editing by Dan Sieck
Cover and text design by Janet Bergin, empoweryourawesomeness.com

The student on the book's cover is the author's son, Tyler Jonas Castro.
He got his hair cut not once, but twice for this picture!
Thanks, Puppy. Love, Mom

Also by Crystal Jonas:

"College Success Your Way: What Your Professors Won't
Tell You and Your Friends Don't Know"
– a book

"Student Success 101:
101 Helpful Hints So That You Can Live
a Rich and Happy Life"

"Student Leadership 101:
101 Quick Tips to Help You Lead So Others
Will Happily Follow"
- also a book

Dedication

This book is for my three children Tyler, Jaclyn and Cameron.

Time goes by so quickly. May you always appreciate its value and your value in this world.

Love you three so.

Letter from the author

Dear Reader,

As a student, you have a seemingly endless list of things to do and people to please. Plus, you are, I trust, applying my advice in my book "College Success Your Way" and using your golden years in school to do the right extracurricular activities and to make the right kinds of contacts so that you can jumpstart your dream job while still in school.

Whew!

How is one person supposed to carry off such a Herculean task?

Simple. First, all you need are powerful yet practical time management tips, tools and techniques. Second, you need to need to consistently use them.

This book, like the others in my "Student 101 Series" is specifically written with you in mind. It's designed to give you a wealth of immediately useful information that you can read and apply quickly.

So read, heed, and reap the rewards of time well spent.

Warmly,
Crystal Jonas

Know How You'll Spend It (Time, that is)

My personal philosophy that I tell college and career audiences across the country is that "no amount of time is enough if you don't know how you're going to spend it."

Here's what this means to you. Without goals, you drift through life without direction. Goals focus your attention and help you structure your time.

You know if you've read my book "College Success Your Way: What Your Professors Won't Tell You and Your Friends Don't Know" that I believe students who have a clear plan to jumpstart their careers while still in school will know exactly how to make the most of their investment of time, energy and money in school.

Make sure you are clear about your values and goals and have a plan for your time. I always say that people who don't have goals work for people who do. Which group will you be in?

Be Willing to Let Go Quickly

You know what stinks? Mean people. Problem is a person can waste a lot of time obsessing over someone else's bad behavior.

Have you ever spent your valuable time wondering what someone else was thinking or reliving an embarrassing situation? Of course you have.

Problem with that is that it sends you into a black hole of major time drain.

Whenever you spend your oh so precious time worrying about what you or someone else could have done differently but didn't, remind yourself that every minute you spent stuck in that unhappy, uncomfortable memory, is 60 seconds you've lost doing something to make you feel good about yourself and others.

Do What Extraordinary People Do

When I give my seminars about "Living an Extraordinary Life" I tell the audience, "When you do what successful people do, you get what successful people get."

Successful people have a clear idea about how they will spend their time.

I know, sometimes you just want to go with the flow and not be held to a tight schedule. That's completely understandable.

Just make sure that most of the time, you have a clear focus and direction so you know what you will have accomplished by the end of your day.

How much of the time should you schedule? Try 80% and see how much you get done. If you're uncomfortable getting that much done, scale back a bit.

I'm thinking you'll like the results.

Manage Expectations

Manage your expectations of yourself, and the expectations others have of you.

Let's say that you have a free Saturday. You don't have to work, you don't have study group, and you've decided this is a great time to catch up on those 500 pages of reading for your History class.

Before you set your alarm for 6 AM and plan to read until 9 PM, do yourself a favor and set challenging, yet reasonable goals for yourself. If you set the bar too high, you will get discouraged and give up after about, oh, three paragraphs.

And while you're at it, let others know what you can do. If your study group assigns you an entire chapter to report on in the next 24 hours, let them know if you will be glad to take the first half of the chapter, but you are booked up past that.

Ok, they won't love it, but it's better than pretending you can get through all of that and discouraging yourself and your group.

Unplug

There, I said it and I'm glad.

In "Mind Tricks That Make Learning a Piece of Cake," a chapter from "College Success" I talk about listening to music that will actually help you study better. Short story, generally it's the classical type. Especially, it's the type without words.

Now, get on the right music, turn off the TV, recharge your cell phone (since you're going to have it off anyway), and for Pete's sake, stop surfing the net, you and I both know what a time sucker that is.

I want you to get really focused when you study so you can study less, remember more, and go have some fun while you're in school.

So stop distracting yourself, get the studying done, and then kick up your heels! You deserve the break.

Practice Selective Procrastination

There's an old saying "It's not enough to be busy, what are you busy about?"

Many wildly busy college students I meet from across the country tell me that they feel as though their schedules are booked 24/7. To see them rushing from class to class, I don't doubt it.

But here's the tough question: Does everything on your 'to do' list really need to be done? Are you doing stuff out of habit? Because you don't know how to say no? Because you're not really sure what you REALLY should be doing, so you're going to do a bit of everything and hope SOMETHING is the right thing?

Well, my friend, you know if you've read my books just for college students how I feel about wasting any kind of time when you're at college.

You should have a clear idea of what you want to get out of college, go for it with a clear focus, and leave yourself some downtime to relax and enjoy the ride.

So next time you feel like you're running around like a crazy person, stop in that moment and ask yourself, what can I NOT do today so that I can do the things I really need to do much better?

And then, procrastinate on those activities that didn't make it to your short list.

Trust me, even if you don't finish every teeny tiny thing on your humongous to do list, the world will still be revolving on its axis tomorrow. And if it isn't, you can blame me.

Study Smarter, Study Less

Yeap-o. You read that right.

Don't study:
Anything you already know
Anything you haven't reviewed quickly first
When the TV is on
When your time is better spent napping
When you're distracted

Better to spend 15 minutes of time with focused studying, than 60 minutes when your mind is elsewhere. Do not even think about wasting your time this way.

Clear your head. Focus. Study. Review. Be done.

Focus on the Prize

Ready for the heresy?

My philosophy holds that the purpose of college is not to get good grades. Ok, ok, before you start the emails, if you're going to grad school, med school, law school, knock yourself out, make that 4.0.

But before you burn this book, or show it to your professor whose class you're flunking and say "See, Crystal is a former Assistant Professor and she says the purpose of college isn't to get good grades," make sure you do quote me correctly.

That's right. The PURPOSE of college isn't to get good grades. The PURPOSE of college isn't to have a good time, either. (Gosh, just when you and I were going to be such good friends.)

My dear friend, the purpose of college is to jumpstart your professional success in this world. To get that diploma and move into a wonderful career that you would not have had if it were not for that sheepskin.

Now the good grades and the great time, those ARE part of what I call "The Plan." Because if you aren't having fun, you'll quit. And if your grades stink, they will kick you out. So, they are part of the plan.

But keep your eye on the purpose. And the purpose is the prize at the end, that terrific career that you set yourself up to get because you had the smarts to use college well and get that diploma.

Write it Down, Make it Real

Listen up. Or read carefully, I should say.

There are roughly a gazillion studies out there that will tell you what I'm going to tell you right here. People who write down specific goals that are measurable are more likely to get them.

What is it about writing goals down that helps so much? Well, since this book is about Time Management, it has to do, in part, with time.

When you write down your goals, and then write down your plan for carrying out those goals, you start to narrow your focus and stay on task a lot more often than if you had spent the day playing it by ear, or as I say, drifting.

So put your goals and plans to achieve them on paper and keep that paper in front of you.

Think of Time as Currency

People are pretty casual with the way they spend their time. They will waste now over 7 hours a day watching TV, and then complain about not having enough time.

For what?!?!

Think of time as money. You have it, you spend it. When it's gone, you're SOL (So outta luck). Ok, the money metaphor ends here, because if you run out of money, you can always do what most broke people do, use your credit card until you're maxed out, but that would be a bad thing, and you already knew that.

So, use time carefully and remember what Benjamin Franklin said, "Do not squander time, for that is the stuff Life is made of."

Tell Yourself the Truth

You already know from Tips #3 and #9 (yes, go back and read them again real quick) that you're going to do what successful people do so you can get what successful people get.

What successful people do is write down their goals and their plans for achieving those goals.

Now, here's the profoundly powerful step that so many people miss. Don't ask me why.

As you go through the day, track your progress. That's right, check off what you've accomplished, and at the end of the day, tell yourself the truth. Did you do those things that really matter?

If the answer is yes, sleep well. If the answer is no, it really doesn't matter how 'busy' you were that day because you weren't busy doing the things you say matter the most.

Only you know the truth.

Face it, learn from it, and you will go to great heights.

Recognize Windows of Opportunity

In "College Success Your Way" I include a chapter completely devoted to the "Nontraditional" Student. "NTs" as they're often called on campus are students who are over 23 years old and entered college after being in the work force.

In many schools, NTs make up over 70% of the population, and my college success programs for them are some of my most requested.

Whether you're an NT with a busy life, or a T with a busy life, you need to know that you will have many windows of opportunity to squeeze in some studying in the course of a day.

Go ahead, think of all the times your time is out of your control. Stand in any kind of line lately? Waited for someone else in the last 24 hours?

Take control back and be ready to whip out those 3x5 cards containing your review notes and study anytime you have one of these windows.

Because we remember what we studied first, and what we studied last, short study sessions can be an important part of learning what you need to learn while still having time for a life.

Ask the Key Refocusing Question

As I write this, I'm 3 days away from delivering one of my corporate programs to help people make the most of their time and manage multiple projects and priorities. Pretty much what you students have to do on a daily basis.

I tell my corporate and college clients that they can count on spending about 28% of their day getting interrupted. Does that sound about right to you?

The problem is, once we're interrupted, it can be hard to get back on task. Some people never do refocus once they're distracted!

You cannot afford to be one of those people.

So, as soon as you're able to extract yourself from that interruption, ask this key refocusing question, "What's the best use of my time right now?"

I trust that you will know exactly what the answer is, or where to find the answer, because you've written down your plan and you know exactly what your priorities are.

Look, no crime in getting interrupted. It's gonna happen. Key is, get back on track ASAP.

Visually Track Progress

As you work on your main plan, and you list the actions you're going to take this week, make sure you're tracking how that's coming along for you.

I carry a little notebook and will check off the item as I complete it. Not only can I tell at a glance how far I've come and how much more I need to do, I get a real kick out of checking things off that list.

I especially like checking things off the list because I know how important those things are to my reaching my goals.

Try this, you'll enjoy it!

Know Your "One True Thing"

hope that if you don't already, you quickly buy into my vision of the real purpose of college.

Once you see college as a golden opportunity to jump-start your career success, I trust that you will create a plan to use your time for maximum return on your investment of time, money and energy.

And once you've done this, I hope that you will move consistently toward getting that dream job.

Your "one true thing" is what I call that action you can take every day to move you one step closer to making that contact, cultivating that relationship, doing well in that internship or class. Do something every day that is consistent with what your big goals are.

Only you know what those goals are, and only you can determine what that action, your "one true thing" is for today. When you're doing it, you'll know.

Let Low Value Slide

Do you sit down at your desk or table to study, only to suddenly realize that, good grief! This desk is really cluttered, I really need to clean it off. And while I'm at it, I should really thin out the papers in the drawers, and would you look at the floor? When's the last time someone vacuumed around here?

Let's admit something to each other. If you're suddenly overpowered by the feeling that you must clean everything in your surroundings, it's quite possible that you are just putting off something big, (your "one true thing" perhaps?) that you really should be doing.

There's a solution to this avoidance factor.

First, back away from the feather duster, housecleaning right now is a low level activity. Just sit back, take a few deep breaths and ask yourself, "What one action could I do right now that would put me on the path to achieving my goals?"

Once you have that answer, you have your "one true thing." And when, day by day, you keep doing your "one true thing," success adds up pretty quickly.

Rack and Stack

Earlier, you read about the real purpose of school, and the fact that the world's most successful people have clear goals and clearly written out plans for achieving those goals.

I read a great book that said there is enough time to do anything you want, there's just not enough time to do everything you want.

Tough fact to face, but the sooner you get it, the sooner you can start looking at the way you use time as an investment or a waste.

When you are planning your week, you will end up with your plans, based on goals and values, and of course, a 'to do' list.

I often see my corporate and college clients putting on their 'to do' lists about twice as many items down than they could actually do. What's the problem in this? Well, possibly nothing. IF, you are honestly racking and stacking these in the order of priority.

Make sure no matter how long that list is, you are always taking care of that "one true thing" each day that gets you closer to what you value most.

Be "Opposite George"

Once upon a time, there was a sitcom named "Seinfeld." It was funny and you could probably catch it in syndication just about anywhere they have TV across the world.

George was pretty much the loser on Seinfeld. He was always saying the wrong thing, and making the wrong decisions. In one episode, he figures that if all his decisions are wrong, and he always gets lousy results, he should do everything the opposite way of how he normally would do it, hence, "Opposite George."

How can you use this to your greatest advantage? Look at your results. Are you getting the most out of your day? Do you end up constantly getting less accomplished than you should? It might be time to be "opposite George" or in your case, "opposite you."

If you've tried studying with the TV on and find you bomb the test every time, it could be time to turn off the TV.

You know that study groups can be a good idea, and you never seem to get anything from yours, do the opposite. Tell them you'll meet them for a snack after the study group, and you go to the library.

If whatever you're doing isn't working, change it.

Be a Groupie

Ok, by groupie, I mean someone who groups like things together.

This is one of the biggest time saving tips you could use.

Here's how it works. Do you need to call two of your professors to set up 20 minute appointments, call your boss to confirm next month's days off, and call a contact your advisor passed on to you to set up an informational interview*?

Excellent! Make all these calls at one sitting.

Need to do some research for your English paper? While you're at the library, also look up that reference you needed for your History paper.

Going to the store to pick up pet food? Well, get your weekly groceries now, Fluffy isn't the only one who needs to eat.

Grouping like activities together can save you hours and hours a week. Yes, it takes a few minutes to plan. But we are talking an investment of minutes to get a return of hours. And you don't need to be an Econ major to know that's just good ROI (return on investment.)

* Informational interviews are a tip I give in "College Success" so you can get in front of high decision makers at the places you think you'd like to work.

Place Things Where You Need Them

Nothing is more frustrating than for a person who wears reading glasses to have to spend 10 minutes looking for a pair of specs each time she sits down to read.

Have you ever sat down to study only to waste a good 10 to 15 minutes, or maybe more getting all of your stuff in order?

It's time to play the "a place for everything" game. That means that if you need a calculator, it's in one place, all the time, and you can count on that. When you're done, you return it right there.

A big tip here, it's worth it to you to have more than one of most smaller items you use all the time. You may even want to have a backpack, or briefcase that has a spot where you keep a second set of reading glasses, a calculator, whatever it is you know you'll need.

This will save you so much time and aggravation; you'll wonder why you didn't do it sooner.

Rituals that Rock

When you do things in the same way each and every time, what happens? That's 100% right, these actions become habits. Soon, you don't even have to think about them anymore, they seem to happen on their own.

To create a study ritual, find a couple of places where you will generally be studying. This could be at your desk in your room, a favorite secluded spot in the library no one knows about, or the cushy chair in your local coffee shop. Doesn't matter. Just make it the same place as often as possible.

Have your materials ready. (Review Tip #20 if you need to.) As you walk to this study spot, picture your end result. The A on your paper, the terrific score on your test, whatever. Now, think back to what you need to do to put yourself into that position to get that desired result.

Take a few deep breaths and prepare your mind to take in and process quickly the information you'll be learning. As you sit down, sit up straight, see the goal, and begin.

Each time you go to study, think the same positive result thoughts, see yourself in your future career, which came about because you graduated from college, which happened because you enjoyed school and did well, and made a good grade on this test you're studying for.

Part with Your Posty Pad

This is an advanced technique, not for the weak, or someone who has an unnatural connection to those little posty pads.

Hey, I like a note that I can stick around my computer as much as the next guy, but here's the problem. Those things fall off. Yes, they do. For one reason, you keep them on your computer for so long, they eventually just loose the desire to stick around.

They not only fall off, they become part of the background. Like the light next to your computer, or that doodad that's been sitting on your desk taking up space for so long.

This is a problem because you lose track of what the notes said. Then, something that should have been done doesn't get done. And if you never needed to do it in the first place, why even write the note to begin with?

A much better time and frustration saver for you would be to have one little spiral notebook, buy them cheapo in the drug store. Keep this notebook in one spot, like that little front pocket in your backpack or briefcase.

Every time you need to make a note of what you need to do, you have one place to capture that thought. This will save you tons of time and keep you from missing important actions.

Be on Time

In "College Success" I mention how this will allow you to avoid one of professors' biggest peeves. They don't care for people who can't make it on time for class.

Once in a while, you say? Hardly ever happens? Well, ok, then. If it truly rarely happens, not a concern of yours. Again, this is something only you can answer.

Do you keep people waiting for you? Do you show up even a couple of minutes late? Why?

Being a couple of minutes late still sends the message that you don't have your life in enough order to be where you need to be when you need to be there. Yikes! Pretty tough language, isn't it? But look, you're not reading this to read the same old stuff you've read before.

Someone needs to come face to face with you, or page to face with you and let you know that being late is NOT ok.

Remember that you'll have the opportunity to make connections and form networks with people that you will probably never have the chance to be around again. And what they think of you matters.

Be kind. Be courteous. Be on time, all the time.

Be There

You're busy. Sometimes so busy, you may wonder how you'll ever get everything finished.

You may find yourself in Biology, thinking about how you're going to finish that English paper. Or in the library looking at your History book while you're thinking about that fight you had with your best friend yesterday.

There's an old saying and it goes like this "Where ever you are, be there."

Kinda silly sounding, but when you think about it, it makes a lot of sense. Any time you're in one spot, thinking about something totally unrelated to what's going on, in that moment, you are wasting your time, effort, and energy.

And these are precious commodities. Apply your attention well and "be there."

Act Now

When I was an undergrad, I had a German professor who would always tell us, "It's later than you think."

No one likes to contemplate the passing of time, unless you're in the world's most mind-numbingly boring class and you're counting the minutes until it's over.

We like to think we've got nothing but time. We can waste all we want, there will be more.

Unsuccessful people never understand that there's a consequence to all this procrastination. Namely, other people who were acting on all those great ideas are now reaping the rewards of breezing through finals week because they were so well prepared, or smoothly moving from graduation into their dream job because they followed my advice on how to jump start your career in my book "College Success Your Way."

Act now. Those who do, win. Those who don't are left behind.

Multitask When It Makes Sense

Reread Tip #19 if it has been a while. This tip is not about allowing yourself to be mindlessly distracted. Rather, it's about combining activities that go well together so you get more done with less effort.

For example, if you like to exercise, take a friend along. You get fun time and your workout at the same time. Hate to do housework? (Who doesn't?) Mentally review your notes from today's or yesterday's class while you clean. Your space will be straight before you know it and you'll be reviewing without taking any extra time out of your already busy day.

Write your vocabulary words for French onto index cards and carry those cards. Next time you're waiting on someone or something, you can use those 5 to 10 minutes to review.

When you combine activities that complement each other well, you get much more done in much less time.

Know Before You Go

College students often ask me the great question: "What's the best way to study smarter instead of harder?"

Who could blame you for wanting to know a smarter, simpler way of doing things? I want you to know exactly how to do as well as you need to do in college to stay in, have fun, and get a great job when you're done.

So trust me when I tell you that not prepping for class is a HUGE time waster! IF you don't read the material ahead of time, and briefly review what you've learned so far before you go to class you are giving up prime study time.

Prime study time allows you to put less into it and remember more.

To you, this means when you read the material before you go to class and review what you've learned so far on your walk to class, you are preparing your mind to more easily take in the new material.

And what does that mean to you? Better grades, less effort.

Don't Get Left Behind

Falling back in school work is the kiss of death. Do whatever you must to make sure this does NOT happen to you. Even a slight lapse is bad news.

You may know from reading my other books that I'm a big believer in staying on top of all your reading and assignments. If, for any reason, you are not prepared for class, GO ANYWAY.

It's a rookie mistake to think because you haven't finished reading your assignment that the best thing is to just skip class. You're far too smart to fall for that one.

School stinks really fast if you start falling behind.

Look, you want to do well, to graduate on time, and to move right into that great job. And for Pete's sake, why not enjoy the whole journey while you're at it?

Well, if you're going to enjoy it, which you deserve to, you need to NOT get left behind.

Burn the "To Do" List

I am not, repeat – not, a fan of the "to do" list IF you do not have already written down, values, goals and plans.

The "to do" list that's unconnected to a bigger picture is just giving you a false sense of security. Sure, you may think you're getting a lot done, but is what you're getting done what really matters?

Can you look back over the last year and say, "Wow! I am so much closer to my big goals?" If not, why not?

Here's what to do. First, write out your values, then your goals, then your plans. NOW, you can write out your action plan for this week.

Make Little Rocks out of Big Rocks

Take that humongous goal that you have, say, become an M.D., and chunk it down into manageable, bite-sized goals. Let's call them goal-ettes.

You might be a Freshman right now, and being 9 or so years away from your career goal could seem insurmountable. But 9 years ago, you could never see yourself at the age you are now, but sure enough, time did pass.

Keep your eye on the prize. When you make the big goal into smaller goals, you have much more excitement and momentum and are much more likely to sustain your focus and use your time well.

Watch the Dessert First Trap

I love the T-shirt that reads "Life is short, eat dessert first." How fun. I don't see any harm in tossing caution to the wind occasionally and eating dessert first.

Do be careful, however, if you have a tendency consistently to do the stuff you want to do first, and leave the stuff you'd really rather not do until all the good stuff is over.

You know exactly why. Because we're human, and we can easily stretch out all that fun stuff until, well gosh, there's just no time at all left for the stuff that we think we'd rather not do, but which really makes the difference in the course of our lives.

So, if you put the goodies before the stuff that's good for you, nobody is going to hunt you down like a wild animal or cast aspersions upon your character. Only you will feel the difference. It will come through in not getting the big stuff you want.

Your choice. Choose well.

Know and Ride Your Energy Waves

Some of us wake up in the morning happy as little jaybirds.

Others wake up in the morning because we have to and want to take a b-b gun to all those happy little jaybirds twerping around.

You don't always have a choice when your classes start, I get it. I remember my first semester of undergrad school. I registered late and had to take Composition at 7:30AM, as in, in the morning, for heaven's sake! Now that's just wrong! Friends don't let friends take Comp before 11:00AM at the earliest.

Know when your high energy times are and do your creative thinking then. That is, if there's a paper to write, use that high energy time.

During the low energy times, do other stuff you have to do, like clean your place, or buy groceries, but don't even try to do brain-intensive work at that time.

Know Tricks about Making Learning Easy

Some tricks about making learning easy include taking notes in the Mind Map® format, reviewing for about five minutes about five to 10 minutes after class is over, and giving yourself "mini-reviews" several times a day.

By the way, if you don't know how to mind map, there are plenty of videos you can find online to help you out; just type in something clever like "Video on how to Mind Map"

Try to avoid long study sessions; they are exhausting and boring.

Do not try to study while also watching TV or videos. Fifteen minutes of quiet review time is worth more than 60 minutes of trying to learn in front of the tube.

Get a study buddy and quiz each other. DO NOT use this method if you're just goofing off. Goofing off is fine, but it doesn't help you pass the test.

Let Others Know Your Limits

Once your friends drop by to talk, it's hard to kick them out of your space.

When they come by, let them know right off the bat that you have time for a 10 minute break, or whatever. This is much easier than trying to hint to get them to leave. We both know there are some people who aren't clued in enough to take the hint!

When this happens, you can ask them if you can regroup with them later when you're done with your deadline, or you can get up and walk with them somewhere and then leave. Many people prefer this "take them somewhere else to leave them method" than to try to kick them out of their study area.

This skill in assertiveness will carry you well into your career, too. People who get the most of the right things done well know how to gently let others know they need to be focused on work.

Face Them, Solve Them, Move On

When it comes to problems, there's one way to go. Spend about 10% of your time defining the problem, and 90% solving it.

It might help to write the problem out so you can understand the elements. Lawyers will often do this.

Also, it will also help to write out the result that you want. And ask (again in writing) what's the easiest, quickest way to solve this problem?

You may not love the best answer. Follow it anyway. Your life will be much easier if you solve this problem as best you can right now, and then move on.

You'll sleep better, and stress less knowing that you have done something to resolve the issue.

Later, if you come across information that you can use to revisit the problem and make the situation better, go for it.

Until that point, move on, already. Obsession is a real time drain.

Watch the Unscheduled Activities Creep

Any plan needs flexibility. I'll be the first to admit that. The problem arises when you have a chance to do something off of your plan, and you take it, then you have another chance to go off course, then another. Then. . .

Well, you get the pattern. It doesn't take too many "just this once" cases until your plans no longer have meaning to you.

Keep track of how often you do go off task, and how much it's costing you. If there are absolutely no negative consequences, it's time to change your plan. Any plan that can routinely be changed without repercussions isn't one that takes you forward with any certainty.

Plan your work, then work that plan.

Know the Urgent / Important Difference

Urgent is a matter of timing. Important is a matter of value.

Urgent is your ringing phone, the ding of "you've got mail," the knock on your door when you're knee deep in a project. Just because someone is calling doesn't mean you have to answer.

When I give Time Management programs to college and corporate groups, I will occasionally hand out those toy sheriff's badges. The point is, you are responsible for your time. You're responsible for how you use it and if you let others waste it.

You and you alone are responsible for the result you get from your use of time.

On the short list of activities in the "important" category are listing out your values, establishing your goals, and planning your time around those goals. This is something you could put off forever and no one would ever come after you for the oversight.

Only the results you have in your life will let you know if you've answered to the urgent or the important on a consistent basis.

Refocus as Needed

If it hasn't happened yet, there will be a time in your life when you feel as if everything is happening at once and you MUST get it all done or else.

Well, you need a reality check, my friend.

Time is finite, after all. You can do anything you want. You cannot, however do everything.

So when everything is coming at you at once, stop.

Take 5 minutes to write down all of the things you think you must do within the next hour. Pick what actions you can take that will make the biggest difference. Prioritize those actions. Do #1 first. Focus for the next 55 minutes, on one priority action at a time.

This fine-tunes your focus and gives you a nice spurt of energy and determination.

Later, not right then because it's not the best use of your time, but later, relax and ask yourself what in your life you can stop doing so you have more time to do what means the most to you.

Spend 10 Minutes Reclaiming Your Life

When it seems that life is on fast forward and you've got so many people to answer to it seems your time is no longer your own, it's time for a brief, yet powerful regrouping exercise.

It's time to remind yourself of your values, goals, and plans for achieving those goals.

Spend time in deep relaxation, and if the only time you get for this is in the shower, oh well. During that time, picture the results of your goals. Imagine that you already are "living the dream." You have that diploma, you have your great job and you are getting the lifestyle you would not have had without your investment in yourself through your college education.

Once you've got that dream set firmly in your mind, work your way back into the plans that will make that dream or goal happen.

Spend about 10 minutes every day assessing where you are right now and where you want to be. You will have renewed energy and commitment that will carry you through even the crazy-busy times.

Track a Semester at a Time

If your school uses a system other than semesters, then use their method of 'time tracking.'

You will have a clearer appreciation of what's expected of you and you will stay on track of all of your responsibilities if you track your time a semester, or grading period, at a time.

The most successful students, and by successful, I mean happy, academically on track, and focused students that I meet from across the country tell me that they track their time a semester at a time.

As soon as they have their syllabus for a class, they log in assignments, projects, and tests. They know exactly what's due when and nothing catches them off guard.

Also, they find this greatly helps with planning major projects, because they can work towards completing the projects by creating many pockets of time when they can spend a few to several hours at a time getting the work done without the strain of the last minute "oh my gosh, I forgot this was due" feeling.

Control the Flow of Info to You

You know what TMI stands for, don't you? That's right, it stands for "too much info." We generally think it when someone is telling a story in five pages that we could have told in a couple of paragraphs.

Too much info tires you out. You don't need it, so as much as you can, control its flow to you.

This may mean canceling subscription to magazines, not reading all of the newspaper, and not surfing the net when you don't need to.

If you need to, tell your friends you're on an "info diet" this semester, and you won't be able to read any e-mail forwards until you're done with school.

Divide and Conquer

As much as you can, share the workload. If you live with others, even one other, divide the domestic duties.

If you're in a tough class, and sooner or later, you probably will be, then join a study group. You've got to put ego aside and make sure that you aren't the smartest person in the group.

If you are, you are wasting your time.

If you are working on a project with someone else, be up front and honest about what you'd like to do because you do it especially well, and ask the other person what she or he does well and would like to do.

In school and throughout life, you are going to want to be playing to your strengths, and doing what you do best as much as possible.

Divide the workload by doing what you do so well as much as possible and working with others to help each other get the job done.

Get Study Buddies at the Right Time

Study Buddies help you put Tip #42 into practice.

As soon as you realize that you could use some extra help with the material, consider forming or getting into a study group.

Ways to do this? There are a few. Ask your academic advisor. Your connection with your advisor is especially important when it come to those more troubling classes.

No ideas from your advisor? Ask members of your intramural team or your sorority or any other club you're a member of. Or, you can ask your professor, or the people in your class who look smart.

Remember that you do NOT want to be the smartest person about this topic in the study group. And you already know that if you aren't learning anything from the group, you must cut the tie and go to Plan B.

Spend No More Than 10% in Analysis

Got a problem? Earlier, I mentioned that obsessing about a problem is a real time drain.

While you don't want to get stuck in what's been called "analysis paralysis," you do need to spend a bit of time defining your problem.

It's been said that you'll want to spend 10% of your time defining the problem, and 90% of the time solving it.

Defining a problem is not complaining about it. It's taking a left brain look at it. Ask, what outcome do I want? What is the easiest (and you decide what makes something the 'easiest') way to solve this problem? What would it take to make that happen?

List the answers. Prioritize the answers. Work on them one by one. Do I need to tell you there won't be a single perfect solution? No, I didn't think so. Do your best. In your heart, you'll know you did the best you could.

Now, let this go; there is living to be done.

Link Life to Your Goals

The order of success is this:

Values. Know what yours are.

Goals. Write them with great detail so they're exciting!

Plans. Whatcha gonna do to get those goodies (goals)?

As you go through the day, with your plans which are based on your goals, and your goals, which are firmly rooted in your values, make sure your actions, which make up your life, are in keeping with what matters most to you.

Seize Unexpected Opportunities

In Tip #36, I caution you to watch the unscheduled activities creep.

The key is to have a plan, yet to make sure that you have enough flexibility to take advantage of truly valuable opportunities.

Say, for example, you have scheduled two hours of library time tonight. Yet, you have just learned that your school is having a special guest speaker at the auditorium at exactly the same time.

Would seeing and hearing this person be a unique experience that would improve the quality of your life? See her, or him.

Yes, I'm suggesting that you pass on your scheduled study time if you have a unique opportunity. After all, you will have chances to expose yourself to experiences in college that you will never have again. Be discriminating, of course, but do savor those special events that being a college student affords you.

So what about that study time you had scheduled? Make it up. Make it up by studying smarter with tips you are learning in here and in my other books.

Life is about balance and making the most of your time and opportunities.

ID Your 20%

In my book "Student Success 101: 101 Helpful Hints So That You Can Lead a Rich and Happy Life" I touch on your "personal prime time" and how to make the most of it.

Successful people know that they get the biggest results from a few key activities. They also know that there are prime times during which they consistently can count on their best work.

You may totally rock at 6AM. If so, by all means, get up, get your work on your toughest subject out of the way before most people even roll out of bed.

Are you a night owl? Well then, help yourself to a late bout of homework.

You will get more done with less effort if you are using your personal prime time to do your toughest assignments. Save the routine work for when your mental and physical energies naturally slow down.

Know Your Result Before You Begin

I often talk about how much you can get done when you know beforehand exactly what it is you want to accomplish.

When you pick up your textbook, know exactly how many pages you'll read and even ask yourself some questions about the information you'd like to gather from your time reading.

When you go to the library to research your big project, have a clear idea of the information you need.

When you go to a study group, bring questions you'd like help with.

And of course, you know from "College Success Your Way" and the chapter on recognizing and avoiding your professor's pet peeves, you will only go to a meeting with your professor when you know specifically when you walk in what you need help with.

Clarity of purpose helps your brain zero in on exactly the material you need, making your time much more productive and well spent.

Schedule Surf Time

Ok, I'm not even going to pretend to suggest that you shouldn't surf the net, watch TV, or play games or do social media on your phone. Most households have been increasing their time on electronic devices though the years and we keep finding new ways to spend more time plugged in!

So, rather than suggest that you don't surf around on the net, etc., I will suggest that you treat fun time with electronics the way you do anything else that you enjoy that gets you no closer to your goals.

Know beforehand how much time you'll spend with fun surfing, and make sure you're logged off when you need to be. 'Nuff said.

Interrupt the Interrupters

Some people love your company so much that they want to be around you as much as possible.

There are worse problems. However, you do need to gently let them know that you would love to spend some time with them as soon as you are done.

Let them know when you'll be done and of course, keep your promise to spend time with them when you said you would.

Now, for the other types who just talk to anyone who will listen, or allow them to go on and on, you need to exercise your assertiveness skills and let them know that it's back to work for you.

If you've been ignoring them, hoping that if you keep reading long enough that they will take the hint and go away, you need to know that there are people who are just clueless. They don't realize that you're ignoring them, and they will keep talking. Tell them, "Let's talk later."

For those people who are just downright rude and wasting your time, you need to be more firm. Say, "I'm going to have to say goodbye now. Time for me to get back to work." Trust me, you won't crush them. These people have thick skins.

Protect your time against well meaning and not so well meaning time wasters.

Call Your Time

When my sisters and I were kids, whenever Mom would take us somewhere, we would race to "call" the front seat. Whoever called it first got to sit up front.

"Call" your time in a similar way. When your friends and or family are talking about what they're going to be doing tonight or over the weekend, make sure you call your time.

It goes something like this: "Saturday, I'm going for a run from 9 to 10, then I'm going to the library until 3:00. Anyone want to go to the movie at 7?" This way, people know that you have a plan and will respect your time more than if you just go with the flow.

Claim your time and allow for time for fun, friends, and family.

Limit the "Pop-In"

Do you have friends or family members who like to pop in while you're studying?

You could be obviously neck deep in books and papers and they will either hover at your door, waiting to be asked in, or come right on in and plop down in a chair near you.

You can let them know right away that you're available at whatever time, as soon as you finish your work, or you can give yourself a break and let them know how long you have.

It goes like this. "Hey Jackie, perfect timing. It's time for my 5 minute break. Let's take a quick walk to the soda machine." You'll recall from an earlier tip that it's easier to take your unexpected guest to a common area and then tell them you need to return and get back to work than it is to kick them out of your office.

Plan the Times You'll Check Email

Who are we kidding? It's easy to get sucked into checking email and social media. I know, we need it. Well, at least we have certainly come to rely on it.

But, how much is really valuable, and how much is simply a distraction?

I tell people in my Time Management classes that before they even open the email or go to their favorite social media site, they should know exactly what their plans are for the day and what the hottest projects are.

It's much harder to be caught off guard and slip into this form of time suck if you know that you are doing a quick scan for the hottest topics and that you will return to most of those messages later when your physical and mental energy are not in "prime time."

Group Like with Like

When you have many things to do, which will be most days, you will save literally hours and hours in the course of a week if you group like activities.

Say you have to call your professor, your girlfriend, and your advisor, you need to write a thank you note for your informational interview (because you're following my advice in "College Success" about jumpstarting your career while still in school) and need to write your sister's birthday card, and you need to go to the grocery store, the bank, and the post office.

Ok, you get the picture. You're going to make all the calls at once, you'll write all the notes at once, and you'll do the errands at once, of course, with their location factoring in to when you do what.

You will love the time you get back in your life when you start to do like with like.

Hide

Especially if you're social like I am. When I was in school, I was the one who would be ready to stop studying at the drop of a hat if I knew some friends were available for coffee or lunch.

I quickly learned that if they couldn't find me, I wouldn't be distracted, so I found this little cubby hole in the library that only the really serious grad students seemed to know about.

It was great! I got so much done in such a short amount of time that I ended up spending most of my last three years at school studying there.

Find your own little get away. And once you do, DON'T tell anyone! It defeats the idea of hiding if everyone knows where you will be!

Watch the Multitasking Monster

There's a myth out there and I take it as my personal responsibility to help squelch it. That's me, Crystal Jonas, "Myth Squelcher".

The myth goes like this: the more things you can do at once, the more time you save and the more productive you are.

First, I want to know who started that rumor. If you know, send that person to me and I'll chastise that person strongly. And you know how much a strong chastising can hurt!

Second, I want you to know that if you are multitasking actions that don't mix well together, you are in a huge time suck. You may think you're making the most of your time and actually you are saving none of it and wasting all of it.

ONLY multitask actions that complement each other. Therefore, you can record your vocabulary words and listen while you workout, or fold your laundry.

Do NOT mix two tasks that require your attention. So, for example, do not even study with the TV on. You will end up distracted the entire time.

ID Prime Time

Look, it's not a character flaw if you're not a morning person, it's just that your body works on its own time clock.

You have natural rhythms of physical and mental energy through the course of the day, and the sooner you learn when you do which work the best, the sooner you can start playing around with your schedule so that you can play to your strengths and make maximum use of your energy.

Just for one day write down what you did when. Yeap, keep a time log. I wouldn't ask you to do it if there weren't a big reward for you, so do it.

This log will help you track how long it takes you to do stuff. Check it out when you're done. Make changes that make sense.

Once you ID your personal prime time, you can get a lot more done with a lot less effort.

ID Time Wasters

Now, before you think I'm being tough and don't want you to have any fun, remember that I'm all about having fun and getting your goodies.

However, how fun is it when something or someone wastes your time and keeps you from taking the steps that are going to get you what you really want?

Remember the time log idea from Tip #57? You're much more likely to control how you spend your time when you're aware of where it's going.

All of us have our own special ways of wasting time. It may be that we like to talk, watch TV, or surf the net for hours on end.

We may even be doing something that feels as though it's productive, but the return on our time investment is quite low. An example of this would be too many hours spent researching before writing a paper. When you've got enough info, but you keep on researching, you're really just procrastinating writing the paper.

So, that time log you kept for Tip #57 will help you realize those time-wasting activities that are neither fun, nor productive.

Indulge

Yes, you read that correctly.

Indulge yourself with your favorite rejuvenating activity (or relaxing activity, for that matter).

Have fun, kick back, do something completely for the fun of it. Not because it gets you good grades, or gets you closer to getting a great job after college, or because it ends poverty. (Ok, if you can indulge in an activity that ends poverty, go ahead and do it, and bless your heart.)

Do your indulgent activity to remind yourself that life is full and rich and wide and you deserve to have balance on your path to cultivating your talents to make the world a better place.

So follow these 101 tips and you'll be using your time well. This includes indulging yourself in some much needed fun from time to time.

Enjoy your indulgence consciously, purposefully, and 100% guilt free!

Leave 'em

True confession, I have less than zero patience for people who tell me they're going to meet me somewhere at a certain time, and then they come late. No phone call, no apology, just late.

Now, if this isn't a pattern, and they do call or are apologetic and have a reason for being late, that's a completely different thing.

You've probably picked up this already. There are people in the world who come late. Why is that? Well, that is another book all to itself, and in the interest of helping you use your time well as you read this book we will have to save that discussion for another day.

Your point here is this. You need to tell them that they need to call you so you aren't left waiting. Or you can have them meet you where you can work, or read, or do what you want to do until they show up.

If they keep being late, it's time for tough love. That means you get up and leave. Don't wait for them. If you continue to wait for them, they will continue to keep you waiting.

And you, my friend, have better things to do with your time.

Plan Meeting Times

You'll want to book office hours with your teachers in advance.

Sure, they might have a set number of hours they're in the office, but they prefer to plan their time. (Good example for us, wouldn't you say?)

If you book your time in advance, you are going to suggest to them that you think ahead, that you're thoughtful, and respectful of their time, and purposeful with yours. Wow, you're really making a good impression now!

While you're at it, make sure you know exactly what you want to ask during your office visit. For example, if there's a concept you're having trouble understanding in class, you can tell the professor what you DO understand, and let her or him know where it starts getting foggy for you.

And remember (from the "College Success" pet peeves chapter) you never go for an office visit because of an 'unexcused absence.'

Get It Right before You Write

Don't like to write college papers? You're in the majority.

Here's what you need to do. Jot down your main idea with about three to five supporting points.

Before you write another word, before you read a single article or spend five minutes in the library, make an appointment with your professor to make sure you're on the right track.

If you aren't you'll know right away without wasting any valuable time. Your professor might even give you some valuable golden nuggets about where to take your ideas.

This is a very good thing. Getting ideas from your prof is a great way to write a paper that she's guaranteed to love.

That tip alone was worth the price of this book, by the way.

Read Smarter, Study Less

Let's understand something. You'll read volumes before you get that diploma. But nobody said it had to take you forever to get all that stuff read.

I suggest you teach yourself to speed read.

Here's what you need to know. When it comes to speed reading, it doesn't matter how many words you read or pages you turn, the point is how many ideas are you getting?

Always start your reading homework knowing:

How far you'll read

What you already know about this topic (do a quick 5 minute review)

What the intro says

What the questions at the end of the chapter say (If there are any)

What's in the tables, graphs, pictures, and bold face.

You still need to read the material, but that little 5 to 10 minute review just saved you tons of time.

Learn How to Mind Map®

Tony Buzan created mind mapping®. That's why there's always that little ® by it.

You can get his book called "The Mind Map® Book" because it will teach you how to visually depict all of that great information you're taking in from all of your classes.

Or you can look up how to mind map on the internet. You will be able to take fewer notes, study less, and recall more the more you use this colorful, creative technique.

It's fun, interesting and useful. Try it, you'll like it!

Be a Quitter

When you're studying, do not even try to pretend that you're going to do a four hour stretch of reading and homework in one sitting.

First, it's BORING! And if you're bored, you won't be learning a thing. Which means what? That's right, you're wasting time.

Second, it goes against what your brain needs to function at peak performance.

We remember what we hear or read first and what we hear or read last. This has been called the "Law of Primacy and Recency." Catchy concept, isn't it?

So, to remember the most from the least amount of effort, study or read NO MORE than 50 minutes before getting up for a 5 minute stretch.

If you're reading technical stuff, go no more than 15 minutes before a quick breather.

Gather Your Goods

Nothing stops the flow of work faster than having to stop the momentum to gather the stuff you need to do the work you want to do.

If you don't love the work, it's that much easier to be distracted, too.

So, you know more than anybody what you need to get your work done.

Do you need a calculator? Colored pencils? 3x5 index cards? Your reading glasses? A highlighter? Then gather those goods and keep them ready in one place.

We waste far too much time looking for stuff, so make sure you always keep your goods in the same place so they are ready for you and you don't have to waste 15 minutes gathering everything.

Oh, and one more thing. If you study in more than one place, and most people do, do yourself a big favor and take the little bit of extra time and the little bit of extra money to buy two sets of everything you need.

You can keep a briefcase or a backpack by the front door in the coat closet with a spare set of all the little things you need when you study.

This will end up saving you from the distraction and frustration of running all over looking for things, or worse, having to go out and buy these things again.

Know There's Enough for What Matters

You have all the time you need to be as successful as you wish to be!

One thing I have learned for sure is that successful people get done tons more than most other people.

So these wildly successful people have accomplished more in one lifetime than many might in five. What are they doing?

Answer: They know what they want, and they know that there IS time to do what matters most.

Do you know what matters most to you? Are you doing what gets you those things?

Then you know exactly what I'm talking about.

Use Drive or Commute Time

Especially if you live in a big city with lots of traffic, or mass transit, you have lots of extra time to make the most of.

Use your phone recorder or some kind of hand-held recording device.

Record yourself reviewing the highlights from your reading material, or from the class lecture. Record your vocabulary words and their meaning. Record whatever will help you review the info while you ride or drive.

This is a great way to expose yourself to important material when you pretty much are stuck going nowhere anyway.

Also, if you have this tape recorder, you can use it to capture your ideas for projects and papers, too.

You never know when you're going to get that brilliant idea. And you've had brilliant ideas before, you know if you don't get them down right away, they're lost forever.

Plan Tomorrow's Success Today

Use your college experience to jumpstart your dream job. And you can start planning for unlimited success right now.

All too often, people wait until the last minute to plan their future. Then, they find themselves one semester, or one month, or even one week away from graduation, THEN they start to think, "Gee, I guess it's time to look for a job."

Ya think?

Use your time in college and your contacts there to plan your future career. Talk with your professors, ask for informational interviews with their contacts, make the most of the activities, clubs, and associations at school.

You will never again have the number of contacts and the level of opportunity that you have to plan the perfect career as you do when you are in college. So, make the most of your time in college and start creating tomorrow's success today.

Sit Where It Counts

can't think of many things that give students a false sense of security more than thinking that just showing up in class is enough.

Yes, it's true, showing up is a good thing.

However, it's not enough. If you aren't prepared for the class in the first place, if you're going to sit in the back and work on your next class, or talk with friends, or just zone out, you're wasting your time.

Prepare by reading what the syllabus tells you to read, and write down any questions you have.

Sit no further than the third row. And sit right smack in the center.

Do this for two reasons. One, because the professor will see your wonderful face, all prepared and ready to learn and will look favorably on you when she grades your paper. Two, because it will help you stay awake and attentive. Both of these conditions are necessary if you're going to do as well as you can in the class

Picture Your Notes

ere's a quiz, in which tip do I mention Mind Mapping®?

Ok, I'm kidding. If I were giving a quiz, that would be an RSQ, (Really Stupid Question) as it in no way tests whether you understand the meaning of the material.

During the seven years I was an Assistant Professor of English at the U.S. Air Force Academy, I made it a point of honor to never ask a stupid question.

The tip I refer to is #64, by the way.

As the cliché goes, 'a picture is worth a thousand words.' This is a cliché that can serve you well. When you develop your own personal shorthand as you go through school, you'll get better and better at creating symbols and pictures to stand for major concepts and ideas.

Since our ability to remember pictures is almost perfect (and how cool is that, by the way?) you will remember far more as you begin to capture the main concepts that you're learning in pictures.

As you do this more and more, you'll get better and better at it. You'll also learn how to visually depict the connections between the concepts you're learning.

Before you know it, you'll be able to put the ideas for an entire semester down on a single sheet of paper and there will be no test you cannot pass.

Develop Your Own Shorthand

This will help you with Tip #71.

As you go through your degree program at school, you will find that there are ideas, principles, and concepts that are referred to often. Start to develop your own personal shorthand for these concepts.

Also, create your own abbreviations for words that are frequently used, or people whose ideas are heavily referred to.

So, for example, if you're taking Psychology 101, you will probably hear about Freud, and defense mechanisms. You can abbreviate these as F and dm, if you like.

Do whatever works best for you. All that matters is that you remember what your abbreviations stand for! And if you're reviewing on the system to study less and remember more that you learned in "College Success," you will remember your shorthand code.

This will save you from writing an unnecessary amount of info during class and possibly missing something that's really important.

Plus, it makes review easier, because there is less fluff to process.

And as you've probably gathered by now, fluff is not our friend.

Don't Overextend

This is true whether you're stretching out for physical activity or booking your schedule for the next month, week, or day.

It's been said that people will overestimate what they can do in a week, and underestimate what they can do in a year.

In the years I've been a national speaker, I've found this to be absolutely true.

You've already read about keeping a time log, not for the rest of your life, but just once in a while so that you can really know how you're spending your time.

Make sure that your schedule is balanced and is full enough to challenge you, but not so full that you consistently can't get it all done.

We all over-schedule at times, not a big deal, but if you consistently are unable to complete the big things, you are overextended.

You need to drop back on what are "B" level priorities so that you can make sure you have time to do what is really important.

Know It Doesn't Matter
How Long It Takes

When I travel across the country delivering my programs for college and corporate audiences, I will often have people come up after my keynote or seminar and talk with me.

When they talk about how much effort they put into a project and how very little it was appreciated, by either their teacher or their boss I can hear the frustration and disappointment come through.

Then, I have to be the one to give them tough love and remind them that how long a project takes to complete is absolutely inconsequential.

Yeap. It's true. Nobody cares how long it takes to do something, they care about the quality of the end result.

So, put your focus on the high quality result you want to achieve and quit thinking that it makes a difference that it took you so long to complete it.

Be the Willow

Ever see a willow tree? It's flexible, so it can bend but not break when the strong winds blow. Yet its roots are strong, and it continues to grow and thrive.

When it comes to time, when it comes to life, even, you be the willow.

Let your roots be your connection to your values, and let your flexible nature allow you to bend, but not break when something unexpected blows through.

This way you will thrive, continue to reach your goals, and maintain your sanity in a world that can sometimes be a whirlwind.

Read with Focus

The very best way to cut down on the time it takes you to read is to cut out all distractions and to read with calm concentration that comes from having a clear goal. What are you wanting to get out of your reading?

You are wasting time if you sit down to read without a clear focus of what it is you'd like to get out of your investment of time.

Read with a plan. How do you develop a reading plan?

Well, of course, it doesn't take a lot of time. Five or ten minutes, tops. Start with reviewing what you already know, then flip through the pages quickly to know how much you'll cover.

Next, read the very beginning and the ends of the chapters. This is especially helpful if there are introductory summaries, and questions at the end. These will help you fine-tune your focus.

Then, you review any charts, graphs, or visual aids after which you read all of the subheadings that are in bold print.

Then you read.

This will help you focus your mind and make reading much faster and much more productive, because it will help you grasp and retain the information better.

And after all, the reason you're reading is to understand and recall.

82   © Crystal Jonas

Speed Read

Here's what most speed reading programs don't teach you. The goal isn't about the number of words read or pages turned.

The goal is to comprehend and retain ideas. Ideas, that's the key.

That's what you need to be on the lookout for. That's what needs to be learned, and that's what will be tested.

Keep this in mind when you put Tip #76 to work for you.

Look It Up Later

English teachers around the country might be cringing as they read this tip, but remember, for seven years I was an Assistant Professor of English at the Air Force Academy, and I still don't believe that readers should stop the flow of reading to look up a word in that very moment.

For the most part, just highlight the word and make a mental note that you will be reading with the intention of finding the meaning of that word.

In "College Success," I mention some reading myths that slow you down. Thinking that every word matters is one of those myths.

Remember that all of the testable concepts are repeated. So, if you don't understand that word, trust me, you will see it again in different contexts and when you're done reading that particular section, you can then go back and look up the word.

Quiz Yourself

College students across the country have told me how much this one little tip that they heard in one of my seminars has saved them time.

Here's how it works. As you study, start with some questions you imagine that you would put on a test if you were the professor of this class.

Review or read with these in mind. After about 15 to 25 minutes, put your material down and quiz yourself. Actually state the answers completely in your head.

It is not, repeat, NOT good enough for you to blow this off and say, well, I know it, I just can't put it into words.

Well, if you can't put it into words, you don't have a firm enough grasp of the material yet.

And since most material in school builds on what came before it, it doesn't make any sense for you to continue to review if you haven't grasped what you've looked at so far.

So stop, quiz yourself, and when you've learned that section, move on.

Review in Ten

Cool thing about how your brain processes information. About ten minutes after you hear it, your memory is at its peak. In other words, in those moments, you know more and can recall more about what you've just studied than at any other time.

It comes ten minutes after the last idea you heard because it takes a while for your brain to process the ideas and connect them to what you already know about the material.

(Since we learn by connecting new material to old material, this is why I encourage you to review what you already know before you ever start adding to that knowledge base.)

So, ten minutes after class, review the material you just heard. This does not require a formal setting, by the way. Review in your head as you drive to work, or walk to your next class, or ride your bike home.

The point is you don't need your notes in front of you to review and to lock this info into long term memory.

Know What You Don't Know Before You Go

You aren't expected to completely grasp every principle in your text books just because you prepared for class. I imagine there are a few people in the world who do read something once and completely understand it and remember it.

However, most people I meet, (and myself included) are not one shot wonders.

So, what this will mean to you is that you want to know which points from your reading you'd like clarified during class.

Do not hold the questions until later. Trust me, if you have those questions, other people do, too. And, it's a waste of time for you to make a separate appointment with the professor to ask these questions.

Now, this is not to say you cannot request office hours, just cover as many questions about the text right there in class.

By the way, one of the three questions never to ask the professor has to do with asking questions when you haven't read the material. So, asking without reading remains a BIG NO NO.

Recognize Gifts of Time

Remember what I said in Tip #1? Go back and read it now, and I'm sure you'll recall the 'take home point' and that's my saying that "No amount of time is enough if you don't know how you're going to spend it."

When you have a plan for your day, and you're prepared to use smaller bits of time to study for a few minutes here and there, then you are ready to recognize and use these gifts of time.

That's what I call those little bits of time here and there, usually when we're waiting for something over which we have no control to happen.

Think of all the time you wait in the course of a week. You wait for your professor to come to class (not often, I hope!). You wait in line at the Student Financial Aid department to ask a question. You wait for a friend who's late for lunch.

You wait a lot, don't you? Well, be ready to whip out those 3x5 cards that have your notes, or your mental mind map of a class you just took.

These count towards study time, you know. You don't have to be sitting at a table with a book open in front of you to be learning.

You can be right there in line at the bank reviewing your world history and no one will be the wiser, no one except you, of course.

Color

When you start to use some kind of mind mapping® techniques to take notes, you will soon begin to realize how easy it is to remember all of those great ideas when you're using color to take those notes.

Color uses more neural pathways (that's just a fancy way of saying color engages your brain) and when this happens you retain and can recall information a lot easier.

So color away my friend!

Mind Map® Your Papers

Before you sit down to write a paper on your computer or with that regulation college-ruled notebook paper, take out a sheet of the unlined printer paper, and use the Mind Map® method to draft out your ideas.

It helps your ideas flow more easily because this method works with how your brain naturally works, which is non-linear.

Need a refresher of this concept? Let me make this fast and easy for you and send you for a quick review of Tip #64 so that info is at your fingertips.

Get an Internship

With some thought and a plan, you can launch your dream job while still in school.

You are investing a lot of time, money and energy into college, so you want to make the most of it.

Remember that the purpose of college is not to make good grades (although it's part of the plan) nor is it having fun (although that's definitely pert of the plan). The purpose of college is to jumpstart your dream job that you wouldn't have ordinarily gotten had it not been for your diploma.

While you're in college, you are in the ideal situation to make extraordinary contacts and have unique experiences that you wouldn't otherwise get to have.

Get with your academic advisor and talk with your professors, and other students in your clubs and organizations, and find out which internship would be best for you, then apply for them.

Build Your Network

Learn everything you can about networking, and put it to use!

Just as you have a wealth of opportunity for unique experiences while you're in school, you have a wealth of opportunity to meet unique and very well-connected people while you're at school.

Many of your professors are incredibly well known and respected in your community, in the country, internationally. Often, they know people in a wide range of businesses.

Recall that having a network means that you stay connected.

This takes much less time than you think, and is a tremendous return on your time.

Of course, you are there for others, too.

Stay Current

Ok, I know, in the real world, there will be times when you have so much coming at you at once you may feel as though you are 'sipping from a fire hose.' And if you haven't quite mastered your time, you may get just a tiny bit behind.

Now read this carefully, once you fully embrace the ideas in this book, and you know exactly what you want and how to get it, you will have time for what you want most.

You will have time for anything you want to do, but you won't have time for everything you want to do.

If you make academics a priority, you will make the time, not find the time, but you'll make the time to make sure that you stay current in your studies.

Getting behind in your homework and projects quickly bites you in the bottom.

Get current, and make it a priority to stay current.

Don't Skip

Do not skip class.

Is there a dire emergency? You must absolutely miss? Ok, miss.

But, there are fewer emergencies that should make you skip than you think.

Skipping not only makes you even further behind, it negatively effects how your professor sees you.

And you know that you need your connections with your professors because they can help you make the most of your college investments.

So show up, look alive, and stay on top of your work.

Join Selectively

I encourage you to join a few clubs, organizations, or associations at school that have members who share your values, goals and plans.

We are the average of the five people we spend the most time with.

If you're spending your time with people who share your values, and have similar goals, you are far more likely to not only achieve your goals, you are more likely to accomplish those goals with much greater ease.

Keep Goals Visual

Going off your plan for success is a time drain.

To keep focused and on the fast track to success, keep your goals visual.

You know my philosophy that the purpose of college is to jumpstart your career success with a profession that wouldn't be open to you if it weren't for your diploma.

One example I offer to make the goal of graduation visual is to keep a tassel hanging over your review mirror, or somewhere that you will be able to see it frequently.

You can also write out your goals daily and write out your name and follow it with the degree designation you'll receive after college, such as B.S. or M.D or J.D.

Break It Up

When you are involved in a large project, whatever that project is school related, or professional, or personal, if it is a big project, you are much better off breaking this up into smaller goals.

This way, you approach each smaller segment with energy, focus and drive. And you have the gratification of frequent accomplishments.

This will help you move forward consistently, which you must do in order to achieve any major goal.

Be sure to track your success as you go and you'll have all the energy and drive you need.

Get It Right the First Time

First of all, let me be clear that I am NOT a perfectionist, few things you do in life need to be perfect.

However, you do need to make sure your work is "good enough." That's a standard that will depend on your personal goals and what your professors consider "good enough."

Whatever that standard is, make sure you get it right the first time. So, if you are going for a B in one of your classes, make sure you do what it takes to get that grade. Don't slack off, get a failing grade and then have to do the whole class over.

It's a big fat waste of time to do anything you choose to do half way. Again, we're not talking about being perfect; we're just talking about getting the job done right the first time.

Get Informational Interviews Right Away

'm a big fan of developing rapport with your professors. They are usually very well connected in the business community and they may know someone who could talk with you about the field you're interested in.

Most college students change their majors more than once. It's a great use of your time to get these "informational interviews" as soon as possible.

Ask these people how they got into their fields and what advice they might have for you concerning what you could be doing right now to jumpstart your career success.

You may find that the career you thought you would love might not be for you after all.

On the other hand, you may get some terrific information that you can take action on right away while you're still in school.

Either way, you win.

Be the Tortoise

You know the story of the race between the tortoise and the hare. The moral is "slow and steady wins the race."

In school, here's what that means to you. You'll have more opportunities than you can count to blow off school and party.

Bad idea.

Having fun, great idea. Having fun when it means blowing off school, really bad idea.

Remember that the goal of college is to get a great career that you couldn't have gotten if it weren't for that diploma. So, you need to do well enough in school to graduate.

Have fun, while you keep a steady pace with the class work. That way, you get the big prize, (that dream job) and you have fun on the journey.

Take 10 (percent that is)

Take notes on only 10% of the class lecture.

Why? That's all you need to capture the main ideas.

Take any more than that and you're likely to miss more important stuff while you're writing down inconsequential details.

Also, you will be a better listener and make better grades as you become more discriminating on what you take notes on.

As an added bonus, you'll have less stuff to go through when you study and having less to study does what? That's right, saves you time!

See "College Success" by yours truly for more tips on this.

Get a Great Advisor

How will having a great advisor save you time?

For one thing, you might never have to take a class that would take forever for you to do well in if you have a close connection to an advisor who just might be able to get you around that requirement. (In "College Success Your Way" I give 12 tips for passing or avoiding altogether a killer class.)

Also, great advisors could give you the 411 on the best professor to take for a class. (And by best, I mean easiest.)

And they can absolutely make sure that you don't take a class you don't need for your major.

They won't be chasing you down, though. You need to take the initiative here to seek them out and stay in touch with them.

Great advisors are worth their weight in gold. Get to know them, and build rapport with them. They will help you make the most of your college investment of time, energy and money.

Get the Goods ASAP

As soon as you know your schedule for next semester, and who your teachers are, mark this down.

Then, sometime before the very end of the semester, ask your future teachers if you could get their syllabus over the net or through e-mail.

You don't want to wait until the last week of school before the next semester, because your teachers will be grading final projects and exams and will likely be maxed out.

Try this about 2 to 3 weeks before the current semester is out.

Let them know you'd like to get a jump start on the reading.

Even if they don't send you the syllabus, probably because they are re-doing it, they will remember you for asking for it and they will look favorably on you.

And this is always good for you.

Always Tell the Truth

Why is this tip a time saver? Because stress and worry cause the average person not to use his or her time well.

Tell the truth because it's the right thing to do. Because it will save you undue stress. And because it's easier to remember.

So, for example, if you forgot your project was due today, don't make up some long story about it. Honestly say what happened, and get your project in as soon as possible.

Messing up from time to time is understandable, forgivable, and forgettable. Telling an "untruth" about it is rarely completely forgiven or forgotten.

Be Kind to Others

If you've never been great at building rapport with others, college is the ideal time to start.

Getting along with others, more than anything else you do, will positively impact your level of success.

Have you ever heard "It's not what you know, it's who you know"? True, to an extent. Building a network of people who like and respect you could shave years off of your success curve.

Be sure to treat others well and take the time to foster genuine rapport with them.

Your reputation is so hard to build up and so easy to break down. Make sure you are on your best behavior with all people. Trust me, the minute you blow it and are unkind, that's when others will hear about you.

So be nice, and be the kind of person others want to be around.

Be Kind to Yourself

Set your standards as high as your personal best.

Be honest with yourself about whether you are living up to that potential.

And when you are doing what you can to live up to your gifts, cut yourself some slack when all does not go well.

Be kind to yourself. You know in your heart if you're doing your best.

Always know that your best is good enough.

It's better than good enough.

It's absolutely just right.

Remember What Goethe Said

And what did this Goethe guy say?

Well, quite a bit, actually. He was rather prolific, you know.

Fun fact to know and tell — most people have a vocabulary of about 5,000 words. Not that that's all the words they know, it's just that that's all they use on a consistent basis.

Shakespeare used about 25,000 words.

And Goethe, well, Goethe used about 50,000 words.

For now, I'd like you carry these seven words from Goethe with you:

"Nothing is more important that this day."

(Yes, that's seven. Admit it, you counted them, didn't you?)

Now, go make the most of this day.

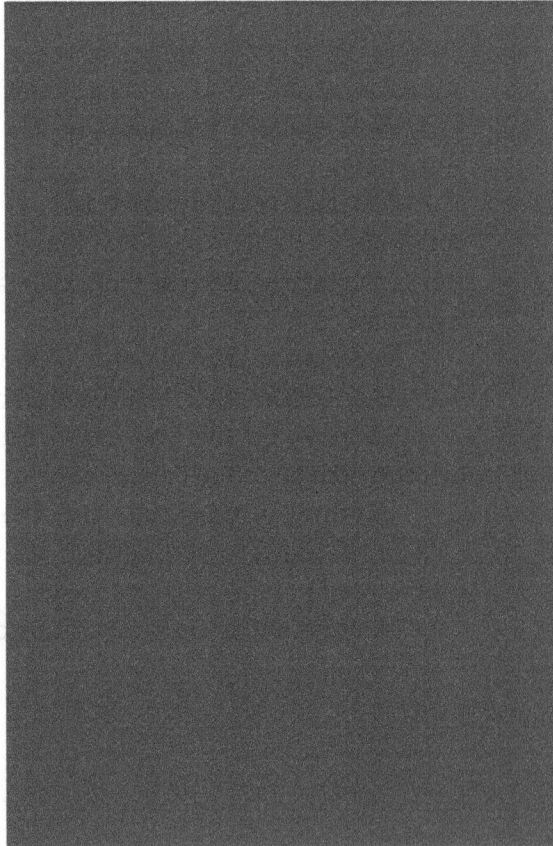

www.ingramcontent.com/pod-product-compliance
Lightning Source LLC
Chambersburg PA
CBHW061755020426
42331CB00006B/1485